THE BATTLE OF THE MARNE

The First Allied Victory of the First World War

Written by Pierre-Luc Plasman
In collaboration with Laure Delacroix
Translated by Carly Probert

History | 50MINUTES.com

THE BATTLE OF THE MARNE   1

Key information

Introduction

POLITICAL AND SOCIAL CONTEXT   3

Tensions between the European powers before 1914

Summer 1914: European powers enter the war

COMMANDERS AND LEADERS   11

John Denton Pinkstone French, British Marshal

Joseph Joffre, French General

Helmuth von Moltke, German General

ANALYSIS OF THE BATTLE   17

The German and French war plans

The invasion of Belgium and the Battle of the Frontiers

The Battle of the Marne

REPERCUSSIONS OF THE BATTLE   30

Trench warfare

SUMMARY   36

FIND OUT MORE   39

THE BATTLE OF THE MARNE

KEY INFORMATION

- **When:** 6-12 September 1914
- **Where:** In the north-east of France, between Paris and Verdun (on both sides of the Marne)
- **Context:** The First World War (1914-1918)
- **Belligerents:** Britain and France against the German Empire
- **Commanders and leaders:**
  - John Denton Pinkstone French, British Marshal (1852-1925)
  - Joseph Joffre, French General (1852-1931)
  - Helmuth von Moltke, German General (1848-1916)
- **Outcome:** French victory
- **Victims:**
  - German camp: approximately 43 000 dead, 173 000 wounded and 40 000 missing
  - French camp: approximately 21 000 dead, 122 000 wounded and 84 000 missing
  - British camp: approximately 3 000 dead, 30 000 wounded and 4 000 missing

INTRODUCTION

The Battle of the Marne marked the first turning point in favor of the Allies on the Western Front during the First World War.

Since the German invasion of Belgium on 4 August 1914, the

Belgian and French armies and the British Expeditionary Force (BEF) had been constantly retreating in the face of the German army. However, the French general Joseph Joffre did not lose hope and launched a major counter-attack against the Germans. The opportunity for this arose when the German general Helmuth von Moltke did not stick to his original plan and allowed space to be created between his armies. From 6 September, a combined action from the British and French allowed soldiers to slip into the breach, threatening the German positions.

The German army was stopped and, on 10 September, forced to begin a general retreat, when they were only 50 kilometers from Paris. They then dispersed north of the Aisne where they began to retreat, marking the Allied victory that was hailed as a miracle by the French public.

The Battle of the Marne put an end to the war of movement and gave way to trench warfare, a symbol of the First World War. Contrary to popular belief, it was these operations in 1914 that caused the greatest losses of the war. The Battle of the Marne was therefore also a disappointment, as the major strategic plans failed and belief in a quick victory was gone.

POLITICAL AND SOCIAL CONTEXT

TENSIONS BETWEEN THE EUROPEAN POWERS BEFORE 1914

The Battle of the Marne took place at the beginning of the First World War. The outbreak of what quickly became known as the Great War was the culmination of a series of causes that date back to the 19th century.

Assassination of Archduke Franz Ferdinand of Hapsburg.

The spark that caused the conflict was the ultimatum launched by the Austro-Hungarian Empire to Serbia on 23 July 1914. This belligerent attitude resulted from the 28 June assassination in Sarajevo of the crown prince, Archduke Franz Ferdinand of Hapsburg (1863-1914), by a Serbian nationalist. This incident, of which the consequences could have remained regional, turned into a generalized conflict, largely due to the play of alliances. This diplomatic and military mechanism functioned like a domino effect: countries went to war with each other as a result of the agreements between them. At the time, two alliances brought together the biggest European powers and aimed in particular to ensure mutual support in the case of aggression:

- The Triple Alliance, created in 1882, included Germany, Austria and Italy;
- The Triple Entente, formed in 1907, brought together Britain, France and Russia.

These alliances were set up gradually due to the political and social context and the tensions that existed between countries. Indeed, each country feared seeing their interests threatened by the others or entering into conflict with them. In the late 19th century, the following could be seen:

- A rise of nationalism. National feelings were exacerbated because countries felt assaulted by others:
  - France wished to take revenge on Prussia after its defeat in the Franco-Prussian War of 1870-1871, and thus to recover Alsace and Lorraine.

- ○ Irredentism, an Italian nationalist movement demanding the land left to Austria-Hungary, was upset by the attitude and actions of Austria in the Balkans. Italy therefore felt frustrated in the Triple Alliance.
  - ○ In Germany, the rapprochement between France, Britain and Russia rose fears of encirclement. Conversely, Pangermanism (doctrine to unite all Germanic peoples and other countries under German domination) and its aspiration for a Greater Germany caused mistrust of Europe.
- The magnitude of the Eastern question (problem caused by the fragmentation of the Ottoman Empire and the resulting quarrel to dominate the Balkans). The Ottoman Empire was becoming weaker, causing not only the independence of the Balkan countries, but also competition between the European nations over the management of public services and the exploitation of natural resources, including oil.

GOOD TO KNOW

The Franco-Prussian war of 1870 resulted from the increasing tensions between the French Second Empire and Prussia, which carried out the unification of Germany by force from 1864. In 1869, following the candidacy of Leopold, Prince of Hohenzollern (1835-1905) for the throne of Spain, Paris called for the withdrawal of this application to the King of Prussia, Wilhelm I (1797-1888). Although he politely refused, German Chancellor Otto von Bismarck (1815-1898) gave a humiliating account of his response, known as the Ems Dispatch, which prompted the French declaration of war on 19 July. The French troops were much more numerous, but the German generals were more experienced and strategic, not to mention the superiority of their artillery as they were equipped with Krupp guns. The French fought successively and Napoleon III (French Emperor, 1808-1873) capitulated after the defeat at the Battle of Sedan on 2 September. The armistice was signed on 28 January 1871, and William I was proclaimed German Emperor ten days later at Versailles.

In the early 20th century, we can see:

- An opposition between Russia and Austria in the Balkan region. Both countries took advantage of the weakness of the Ottoman Empire to expand their areas of influence and gain sea access in the south. Indeed, Russia saw itself as a protector of the Slavic people, especially Serbia, while Austria did not like the Serbian nationalism which animated the Slavic minorities within the empire and threatened their stability.
- Tensions developed between Germany and France over colonial issues, particularly around those relating to Morocco. Germany tried to curb French expansion in this region. In addition, it provided support in 1902 to the Boers (descendants of Dutch settlers in South Africa) when Britain conquered their two states by force.
- The growing economic competition during the Second

Industrial Revolution. The differences between the industrial nations were reduced and the search for new markets pitted Britain and Germany against each other in the Near and Middle East.

- An arms race. Germany launched a naval program in 1900 to compete with the Royal Navy, while France adopted the law of three years in 1913, increasing the length of military service in order to mobilize the same number of soldiers as Germany.

SUMMER 1914: EUROPEAN POWERS ENTER THE WAR

The idea that a war could break out was not feared by the future belligerents as they kept in mind the Napoleonic Wars (1803-1815), which were relatively short and not very deadly.

They had no idea of the magnitude of the destruction that a general conflict could generate in the early 20th century.

All of these tensions led to the idea that a war was inevitable, and could even be beneficial, being rooted in public opinion and the ruling circles – particularly in Germany. Acceptance of an armed conflict was thereby facilitated when the July crisis was triggered. However, the war was not really expected: July 1914 was not a boiling point and nationalists calling for arms remained very few. Indeed, in the past, Europeans had managed to agree in order to prevent conflicts, such as during the Berlin Conference (1884-1885) on the colonization of Africa, or the Hague Conventions (1899 and 1907) that helped to regulate the right of war. Nevertheless, during the summer of 1914, the statesmen and diplomats proved quickly overwhelmed by the events and followed them without being able to influence them.

GOOD TO KNOW

The Hague Convention, or the International Peace Conference, met for the first time in 1899 at the invitation of Russian Tsar Nicolas II (1868-1918). They aimed to disarm and prevent conflict. Some weapons or warfare techniques – such as bombing, poison gas and exploding bullets – were prohibited. The Permanent Court of Arbitration (for resolving international disputes) was also created, but the national powers did not utilize it. A second conference was held in 1907 at the invitation of U.S. President Theodore Roosevelt (1858-1919), which established the obligation to issue an ultimatum before the outbreak of conflict. Humanitarian law, outlined in the Geneva Convention of 1864, was a basis for these conferences.

After the Sarajevo assassination, the Austrian staff saw an opportunity to definitively subdue Serbia. However, Austria did not wish to act without the support of Germany. Germany agreed and encouraged Austria, as it aimed to consolidate it as a main ally, and feared its disintegration. In addition, William II (King of Prussia and Emperor of Germany, 1859-1941) firmly believed in the superiority of his army and in the absence of British intervention. He said that the war would be short and limited. Therefore, on 23 July, Austria issued an ultimatum to Serbia. The unacceptable conditions put forward could only have had one outcome: rejection.

Three days later, Britain tried to set up an international conference to settle the Austro-Serbian dispute, but Belgrade was bombed on 28 July. The war had just begun. Russia, which could not leave Austria to control the Balkans, therefore urged the Tsar to mobilize the troops. After some hesitation, he agreed. The logic of the alliances was then brought into play. Germany requested that Russia turn back, but Russia refused: Berlin gave the order of mobilization in turn on 1 August and Germany declared war on Russia. Furthermore, the German Empire showed itself ready to expand its territory into the East. Immediately, Paris gave the order of general mobilization and awakened its ambition to free Alsace-Lorraine, which was then in the hands of Germany. In response, Germany declared war on France on 3 August. The following day, German troops attacked Belgium and the violation of its neutrality marked Britain's entrance into the war, which could not accept such a disruption of the equilibrium of Europe. Italy, disappointed by the Triple Alliance, declared itself neutral and would re-join a year later, on the side of the Triple Entente.

COMMANDERS AND LEADERS

JOHN DENTON PINKSTONE FRENCH, BRITISH MARSHAL

Portrait of John Denton Pinkstone French.

Sir John Denton Pinkstone French was a British marshal. Like his father, he enlisted in the Royal Navy, but he joined the cavalry soon after, in which he became a brilliant officer. He served mainly overseas: in Egypt, Sudan and India. He stood out particularly during the Boer War (1899-1902), where he participated in the capture of Pretoria (administrative capital of South Africa). In 1907, he was made inspector general of the army and became leader of the Imperial General Staff in 1912. The following year, he was promoted to the rank of field marshal.

Before the First World War broke out, he promoted links between the Allied powers by participating in major French maneuvers (annual military exercises that involved numerous soldiers) and inviting French and Russian delegations to the British maneuvers in 1913.

Appointed to command the British Expeditionary Force (BEF) early in the war, he received instructions aiming to maintain autonomy of action with regards to the French. During the retreat in August 1914, relations with the French general Charles Louis Marie Lanrezac (1852-1925) were strained, as the latter did not support his decision to move back. The BEF, deployed in the region of Mons (Belgium), had to contain the German advance alone and managed to delay it for a while. Doubting the abilities of the French leaders, he decided to repatriate the BEF, but the War Minister Lord Kitchener (1850-1916) refused and John Denton Pinkstone French was forced to take part in the counter-attack of Joseph Joffre on the Marne. In December 1915, he was asked to resign, partly due to differences of meaning with subordinates and with the government in London. He was knighted and made Viscount and Earl of Ypres in 1918 and was appointed Lord Lieutenant in Ireland two years later. He retired from office in 1921 and died four years later.

JOSEPH JOFFRE, FRENCH GENERAL

Portrait of Joseph Joffre.

Joseph Joffre was a French general. A polytechnic student, he took part in the defense of Paris during the Franco-Prussian War of 1870-1871 before participating in several colonial campaigns. Appointed Chief of General Staff in 1911, he promoted the creation of permanent staffs and focused on the improvement of services behind the frontlines and mobilization plans.

Commander of the armies in the north and north-east in August 1914, he avoided encirclement by making a strategic retreat and his counter-attack on the Marne allowed him to stabilize the front. To achieve this, he did not hesitate to frequently visit his subordinates and to fire those he considered incapable. Crowned with the title of "victor of the Marne", he became commander-in-chief of the French armies at the end of 1915 and still believed in the success of an offensive breakthrough. However, his plans of attack failed in Artois and Champagne. In addition, he failed to anticipate the German response in Verdun in 1916. As his whole character earned him growing hostility, the human cost of the battle rested on his shoulders. His disgrace came at the end of 1916 after the failure of the offensive on the Somme. He was replaced by General Georges Robert Nivelle (1856-1924), but he was promoted to marshal of France. Then a military adviser to the French government, he led several missions overseas, including one in the United States to prepare for the arrival of the U.S. troops in France. On 14 July 1919, with Marshal Philippe Petain (1856-1951), the successor of Robert Nivelle, he opened the victory parade. He was elected to the French Academy in 1918 and died in 1931.

HELMUTH VON MOLTKE, GERMAN GENERAL

Portrait of Helmuth von Moltke.

Helmuth von Moltke, also known as Moltke the Younger, was a German general. His uncle, called Marshal Helmuth von Moltke the Elder, was the military architect of the

German unification and the defeat of France in 1870.

He joined the infantry and was moved to the General Staff in 1880. He became the aide-de-camp of William II and managed a division for some time before returning to the General Staff. In 1906, he took command and succeeded General Alfred von Schlieffen (1833-1913), from whom he largely took the plan for the invasion of France.

In early 1914, he believed that the moment was favorable to start a war and pushed William II to militarily exploit the crisis resulting from the assassination of Franz Ferdinand of Hapsburg. However, as war chief, Helmuth von Moltke lacked assurance and his headquarters in Luxembourg were too far from the front for him to be properly informed. In addition, he transferred two armies to the Eastern Front before the attack on the Marne. Even worse, he did not actually direct operations, leaving considerable autonomy to subordinates who committed even more errors. In early September, the uncoordinated German generals left a breach open between their armies, thus allowing the attack from the French General Joseph Joffre.

In fact, his command was withdrawn on 14 September 1914, even though General Erich von Falkenhayn (Prussian War Minister, 1861-1922) did not officially take office until November. He was then appointed head of the internal forces. He died of a heart attack in 1916.

ANALYSIS OF THE BATTLE

THE GERMAN AND FRENCH WAR PLANS

Given the pre-war tense atmosphere and mistrust, the German and French headquarters did not wait for the summer of 1914 to construct their plans of attack. However, these strategies had been designed to carry out a short and quick war, as they were made before the First World War began. The most important offensive plans were:

- The German Schlieffen Plan. The most elaborate tactic was that of Marshal Alfred von Schlieffen, who was considered one of the brightest military minds of his time. Designed from 1898, the plan was to defeat France in a few weeks before turning against Russia, which was thought to be slower to mobilize. The marshal recommended that the German armies form a powerful marching wing that would cross Belgium and bypass the French army before encirclement. By following this plan, the German armies were arranged in August 1914. The 1st and 2nd German armies – which contained almost 600 000 men – thus formed the marching wing, which Belgium was not in a state to resist with its 117 000 soldiers. In theory, they should have begun a turning movement after passing the French army in order to encircle it by trapping it at the borders of Germany and Switzerland. The 3rd and 4th imperial armies were to attack via the south of Belgium and Luxemburg. Finally, the 5th, 6th and 7th armies were to defend Alsace and Lorraine.
- The French Plan XVII. Adopted in April 1913, it was de-

signed by the assistants of Joseph Joffre to conduct an offensive and was the 17th plan developed by the staff. In the early 20th century, French military doctrine focused on the moral strength and courage of the troops to carry out the attacks. Indeed, the fire power had never been greater and the generals were convinced of the superiority of the attacker over the defender.

- The French strategy was therefore simple and aimed to win a decisive battle in Lorraine. To do this, the army had to move in two directions – left to the north of the Verdun-Letz line and to the right between the Vosges and Moselle – before meeting to deliver the final blow. Only the 5th Army stood to the left of the device to guard against a German attack through Belgium.

It is likely that the opposing parties knew the outline plans of their opponents, but it was estimated by the French that the German forces were not numerous enough to achieve their maneuver.

While the beginnings of preparations were favorable for both sides, unexpected events came to disturb the initial plans: the Germans were attacked faster than expected by the Russians and observed Britain's entrance into the war with concern; the French failed in their attack on Alsace-Moselle and saw the arrival of the 1st and 2nd imperial armies through Belgium.

THE INVASION OF BELGIUM AND THE BATTLE OF THE FRONTIERS

To the surprise of Berlin, Belgium - a neutral power - rejected its ultimatum. In defense of the territory, three fortified cities - Antwerp, Liège and Namur - protected not only the rivers, but also the country's roads and railways. Added to this was the systematic use by the Germans of a new howitzer, whose caliber measured 420 millimeters, better known as the "Big Bertha".

German army in Belgium.

On the marching line of the 2nd German Army, Liège and Namur fell respectively on 17 and 24 August. The rest of the Belgian army then retreated to Antwerp. This is when Helmuth von Moltke committed his first mistake. Concerned about the situation on the Eastern Front, he decided to transfer two army corps to fight the Russians. In addition, three other divisions were detached: one to contain the Belgian army in Antwerp, one to occupy Brussels and a final to besiege Maubeuge. The powerful marching wing was amputated of a seventh of its military force.

For his part, the French General Joseph Joffre did not care about events that concerned Belgium, as he was too busy with the preparations for the offensive in Lorraine. On the 14 August, two armies were launched towards Sarrebourg (Moselle), while another two were sent towards the Ardennes on the 22 The British Expeditionary Force, composed of 100 000 professional and well-trained soldiers, landed in France between the 11 and 17, then went to Belgium where the Germans became aware of their presence around the 22.

The battle of the borders thus began and took place in four distinct places of intervention: in Lorraine, the Ardennes, Charleroi and Mons.

- In Lorraine, the French 1st and 2nd armies advanced rapidly to Germany and reached Sarrebourg on the 18 August. However, the German forces were underestimated and, although they retreated, this was only to form a compact block. Superior in number and possessing better artillery, the 6th and 7th German armies carried out an attack on the 20 August and crushed the French, who surrendered three days later on the Meurthe River (Lorraine). In turn, the Germans then committed an error by continuing the offensive. Contrary to what Alfred von Schlieffen had advocated, Helmuth von Moltke allowed the continuation of the attack, which failed in the face of the French entrenchment along the river.

- On the 21 August, the 3rd and 4th French armies were ordered to attack from the Ardennes towards Arlon and Neufchâteau. Facing them were the 4th and 5th German armies, which had the same size force (eight divisions), but had the advantage. Not only did the forest area not lend itself to the attack, but the movement of the French army was also spotted, whereas the French army did not know where their enemies were stationed. Arranged in levels, the French corps exposed its left flank to attack and if the northernmost body was to collapse, the entire device would be dislocated. This is precisely what happened on 22 August. The losses were considerable: the colonial body, the most experienced of all, lost 11 000 of its 15 000 men in bayonet charges that occurred in the forest, against heavy fire from machine guns. Plan XVII was a failure, but Joseph Joffre requested that the offensive continue. Nevertheless, on 24 August, the 3rd and 4th armies retreated behind the Meuse.

- Meanwhile, the 5th Army of Charles Louis Marie Lanrezac unfolded between Charleroi and Dinant (Belgian cities), in the angle formed by the Meuse and Sambre. It had to get in touch with the 4th Army and the BEF that was heading to Mons. However, they failed to seize all the bridges over the Sambre and the Germans infiltrated. The French general then ordered them to return to their positions, but this decision would end in failure: the losses were significant and the French were pushed back 11km. Contact with the 4th Army was therefore broken, while the junction with the BEF had not been achieved.

Charles Louis Marie Lanrezac decided to withdraw in the evening of the 23 August, without warning his British counterpart, John Denton Pinkstone French, who was protecting the left side of the 5th French Army.

- The BEF was deployed along the Mons-Condé canal and British soldiers, with the experience of the Boer War, dug trenches and used their repeating rifles with dexterity. They held their positions, but eventually had to withdraw for risk of being encircled. On 26 August, in the French municipality of Le Cateau, the 2nd British Corps faced 140 000 German soldiers and the BEF lost nearly 10% of its men.

THE BATTLE OF THE MARNE

The German error

The first three weeks of the war were marked by notable successes for Germany, as all the French armies retreated. However, soldiers from both sides were greatly tested by the fighting, the heat, the forced marches and hunger. Moreover, as the Germans advanced into French territory, they moved away from their lines of communication and supply was made more difficult. The situation was different for the French, allowing Joseph Joffre – who managed to stay calm – to concentrate more troops and create new armies. However, dissatisfied with his subordinates, he did not hesitate to dismiss Charles Louis Marie Lanrezac and Pierre Xavier Emmanuel Ruffey (1851-1928), as well as nine generals from the general corps and 33 divisionals.

Despite the many difficulties, the German armies advanced

to France: the 1st Army of Alexander von Kluck (1846-1934), the 2nd of Karl von Bülow (1846-1921) and the 3rd of Max von Hausen (1846-1922) were placed between Verdun and Amiens. On 2nd September, the vanguards reached Meaux, 50 kilometers from Paris. That same day, the French government left the capital to take refuge in Bordeaux and left General Joseph Gallieni (1849-1916) to defend the City of Light.

Simultaneously, Helmuth von Moltke ordered Alexander von Kluck to align himself with Karl von Bülow's army to cut the road to Paris. Believing the Franco-British troops to be in disarray, Alexander von Kluck pursued the 5th Army and the BEF. However, by taking the direction of the southeast, he deviated from the Schlieffen Plan that involved encircling Paris from the west and, without knowing it, strengthened the position of Joseph Joffre. A breach was thus created between the army of Alexander von Kluck and Paris, in which the French General could set up troops transferred from Lorraine – the new 6th Army – to attack the flank of the German army. In addition, in their progress towards the Marne, Alexander von Kluck distanced himself from the army of Karl von Bülow and created another breach in the Cherly-Petit-Morin region. This situation that quickly became critical can be blamed on Helmuth von Moltke and the autonomy that he wanted to grant to his army chiefs, whereas the operations of the Great War required excellent coordination, which he could not deliver from his general position in Luxemburg.

Preparations for the battle

The downturn of the German movement did not go unnoticed and Joseph Joffre gathered the BEF, the 5th and 6th armies and the garrison of Paris in the west of the city. To the right of the device, he stationed the new 9th Army, entrusted to General Ferdinand Foch (1851-1929). Nevertheless, the participation of the BEF remained uncertain. Indeed, John Denton Pinkstone French sent a telegraph on 31 August to the War Minister Lord Kitchener, detailing his intentions to repatriate the BEF in Britain due to the loss of his confidence in the French generals. Immediately, Lord Kitchener went to France and used his influence to force the British marshal to cooperate with Joseph Joffre.

The French chief decided to attack on 6 September. The plan was as follows: the 6th Army had to cross a tributary of the Marne, the Ourcq, to attack the 1st Army of Alexander von Kluck from behind. Meanwhile, the 5th and 9th Armies, with the help of the BEF, should halt their retreat between Meaux and Cézanne. The BEF and the 5th Army would attack, in order to expand the space between the 1st German Army and that of Karl von Bülow, while the 9th Army would stop that of Max von Hausen in the marshes of Saint-Gond (southwest of the Marne).

The day before, Helmuth von Moltke also delivered his orders and admitted the failure of the encirclement. The armies of Alexander von Kluck and Karl von Bülow were assigned to a defensive position in front of Paris, while that of Max von Hausen was to progress downstream of the Seine. The 4th and 5th Armies would attack in the southeast, to allow the 6th and 7th armies to cross the Moselle and complete the encirclement of the French.

In theory, the first days of September were the most crucial for the Germans as they were supposed to achieve victory on the Western Front. However, on the ground, the German armed positions were the exact opposite of those intended under the Schlieffen Plan.

Fierce fighting

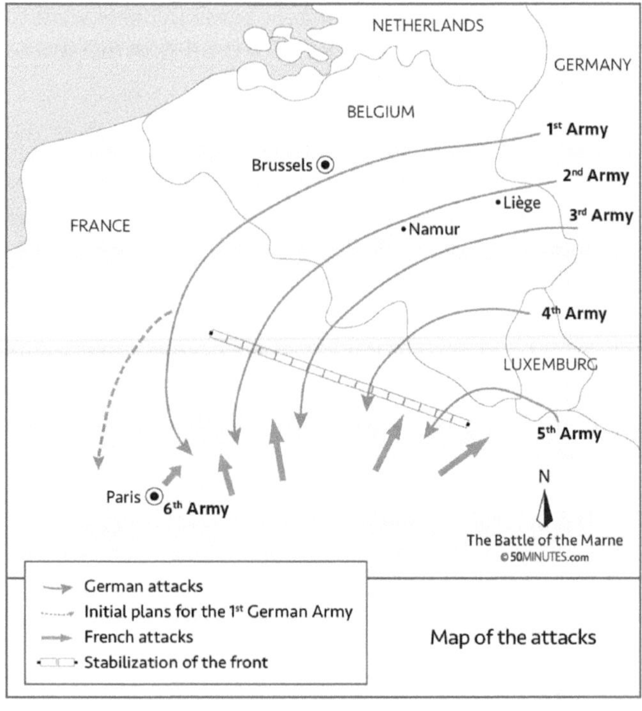

Map of the attacks

The battlefield stretched almost 200 kilometers, where over a million men clashed in each camp. The outcome remained undecided until 8 September:

- In the east, the 4th and 5th German Armies attacked Nancy and Verdun, but the German Emperor witnessed the defeat of his troops;
- Meanwhile, the 6th Army of French Marshal Joseph Maunoury (1847-1923) aligned with the rear of the 1st opposing army, whose troops were more experienced than the French, consisting mainly of reservists. The German general continued to counter-attack and prevented the French Marshal from gaining ground. On 7 September, 600-700 taxis requisitioned by Joseph Gallieni deposited between 4 000 and 6 000 soldiers from the garrison of Paris on the front. This contribution was not decisive, but the episode of the "Marne taxis" is now a story of legend and contributed to the symbol of the French Resistance;

Marne taxis.

- Although in the evening of the 8 September, Alexander von Kluck believed he could circle the 6th French Army, he became completely detached from the army of Karl von Bülow. But, on the 7 Spetember, von Bülow reorganized his device and switched his right wing to the north. Now, the three German armies were separated: Alexander von Kluck was north of the Marne, that of Karl von Bülow was south of the river and that of Max von Hausen was in the marshes of Saint-Gond;

- In the marshes, the 9th Army of Ferdinand Foch was in charge of repelling the German army beyond the Marne. The fights that occurred on 6 and 7 September were fierce, but came to no result. The German general, convinced that the French were weakened, launched a bayonet attack before dawn on the 8 September in order to push the French back five kilometers. Following these events, Ferdinand Foch wrote the following message which later became famous: "My centre is giving way, my right is retreating, situation excellent, I am attacking" (Foch 1920, p. 361);
- The next day proved decisive. With the help of reinforcements from the 5th Army, Ferdinand Foch restored the situation and even managed to launch a counter-attack. The army of Alexander von Kluck, which was separated from that of Karl von Bülow by almost 65km, retained the initiative and could still encircle the army of Joseph Maunoury. The advantage was on the German side, but at 2:00pm, the attack was interrupted by an order to retreat.

The order to retreat

Indeed, the day before the German General Helmuth von Moltke had sent Lieutenant Colonel Friedrich Heinrich Richard Hentsch (1869-1918) to be informed of the situation. Karl von Bülow told him that his difficult position could be exploited by the French and British armies and recommended a withdrawal of the most advanced positions beyond the Marne. The next day, Karl von Bülow warned the other German generals that he was beginning to withdraw. Therefore, they had no other choice but to follow suit and

Helmuth von Moltke had to realign his defenses and have the 4th, 5th and 6th Armies retreat. Over nearly 400km, the Germans fell back by 50km, creating new frontlines behind the Aisne and between Verdun and Noyon.

The losses from the Battle of the Marne alone are difficult to assess. The number of 250 000 killed in the French camp includes the conflict, but also the battle of the borders. Some historians, however, have attempted to estimate the victims and argue that:

- in the German camp, there were approximately 43 000 dead, 173 000 wounded and 40 000 missing;
- in the French camp, there were approximately 21 000 dead, 122 000 wounded and 84 000 missing;
- in the British camp, there were approximately 3 000 dead, 30 000 wounded and 4 000 missing.

REPERCUSSIONS OF THE BATTLE

TRENCH WARFARE

The Marne, an unfulfilled victory

The first months of the war were the deadliest, with an average of nearly 60 000 deaths per month. At the end of 1914, the BEF had lost almost 80% of its forces, forcing Britain to impose conscription (i.e. the obligation to serve in the army). Almost all the active French officers had been decimated. Therefore, it is incredible that we still speak of the "miracle of the Marne" today. The term, subsequent to the event, was used for the first time in an article by Academician Maurice Barres (1826-1923) in December 1914. Although the term was interpreted literally by Christian circles, it reflects primarily the relief of a population in the face of an unexpected turnaround of the situation.

On the field, Joseph Joffre believed in the possibility of a decisive victory by bypassing the German army on the right near Noyon and cutting off its supply lines. But the Germans, trained to quickly create trenches, modified their positions and were now located behind the Oise and the Aisne. Their defensive system consisted of several lines of trenches, connected by communication saps and protected by barbed wire in front of them. The fortification of the new German positions was the last order given by Helmuth von Moltke, but the strategic withdrawal started by his subordinates proved fatal.

The race to the sea

Although exhausted from fighting on the Marne, the Franco-British troops still launched an attack on the German positions and were broken on their defenses. Their situation was made all the more critical as ammunition was running out. Gradually, it became clear that trench warfare would define the Great War. After the first Battle of the Aisne (14-18 September) and during the month of October, each side tried to attack the opposing army from behind. These attempts made by the German right and the French left wings stretched the front to the North Sea. Even though the purpose of these operations was not to reach the sea, it took the name of "the race to the sea".

The Battle of Ypres and the stabilization of the front

The front was stabilized from the Swiss border to the North Sea and the trenches allowed the armies to spare their forces, in order to bring new troops in for an assault. The battlefield moved to Belgium in the region of Ypres.

German General Erich von Falkenhayn wanted to put an end to the Belgian army that was protected by the fortress of Antwerp and, on 1 October, the outer defenses fell. Two days later, no less than 12 000 Royal Marines arrived as reinforcements. The sending of this contingent was the idea of Winston Churchill, First Lord of the Admiralty (1874-1965), who went personally to the Antwerp metropolis. Yet, the city capitulated on 9 October and the Belgian army retreated behind the Yser. It was joined by the Franco-British forces in order to stop the German armies. Erich von

Falkenhayn wanted to both create a breakthrough to take Paris and force France to bend and to capture the other ports and prevent the arrival of British reinforcements. The Belgian divisions were reduced to 60 000 men, yet they managed to keep an area of 15 kilometers, but they lost one third of their fighting forces. Under the orders of King Albert I of Belgium (1875-1934), the engineers opened the sluices in Nieuwpoort (coastal city of Belgium). On 29 October, the plains of the Yser were flooded, forming a temporary line of defense between Nieuwpoort and Diksmuide (Belgian cities). However, the fighting continued to rage in the region of Ypres between the armies of John Denton Pinkstone French and Ferdinand Foch in the 6th German army. Once again, the German artillery proved daunting, although the British rifle skills were just as deadly. The situation was unfavorable for the Allies until 10 November. However, floods, rain, snow and exhausted troops led to the abandonment of the German offensive on 13 November.

Therefore, the front lines hardly moved until 1918 and the Western Front would be marked by other battles, such as those of Verdun (February-December 1916), the Somme (July-November 1916) and the Aisne (April-October 1917).

Good to know

The battles of Verdun, the Somme and the Second Battle of the Aisne are three major offensives that remain in the collective memory of the fierceness of the battles of the First World War.

- The Battle of Verdun was a German offensive that

began in February 1916 and ended in December of the same year. Approximately 300 000 French and German soldiers were killed in a fight that was hitherto of unprecedented violence.

- The Battle of the Somme was a Franco-British offensive which took place between July and November of 1916. For six weeks, Allied forces gained minimal ground, without managing to make the German front yield. As of August, their objective was to maintain strong pressure on the opposing army. The toll was heavy: the Germans lost about 650 000 men, the British lost 420 000 and the French lost 195 000.
- The Second Battle of the Aisne was an offensive launched by General Robert Nivelle on 16 April 1917 in order to achieve a breakthrough to break the stagnation of the trenches. The attack was a disaster – there were about 35 000 deaths in one week – but the French general was stubborn and refused to give up. Riots broke out in the ranks and repression was very strong. Given the catastrophic situation, Robert Nivelle was replaced by Philippe Pétain, who initially focused on improving the situation of the troops. This eventually led to a coordinated offensive in 1917, which led to the victory of the Malmaison on 25 of the same month.

War crimes

On 12 September, at the end of the Battle of the Marne, Reims was taken over by the French, but the city was subjected to bombardment for several days, which killed 700 civilians. In contravention of the laws of war, the German artillerymen did not hesitate to deliberately damage the Gothic cathedral where the kings of France had been crowned. This act brought further proof of Teutonic barbarism to Allied propaganda, as historic buildings, witnesses of history and culture, were legally considered inviolable.

Soon, the First World War represented, in the eyes of the people of that time, a struggle between civilization and barbarism. Britain took part in the conflict, not because it jointly participated in the Triple Entente, but because Germany had violated international law by attacking Belgium. The idea of a "Poor Little Belgium" was very successful and the mobilization of minds through propaganda was almost as intense as the fighting.

Undeniably, the Germany army committed atrocities in Belgium in 1914. Surprised by the resistance of the Belgian army and under the influence of a very hot summer, the Germans' stress only increased and strengthened the fear of coming under fire from francs-tireurs, as in 1870. Believing they were being attacked by civilians, the units committed irreparable acts in the first days of the war. 211 people were executed in the Ardennes, 384 in Tamines and 612 in Dinant. On 25 August, the university town of Louvain – including its rich library – was burned down.

In 1915, the execution of Edith Louisa Cavell (1865-1915), an English-born nurse involved in the Belgian resistance, raised general indignation and promoted the British recruitment program. Germany was also trying to win victories in the propaganda struggle by denouncing the execution of the Irish Consul Roger Casement (1864-1914), who had negotiated the logistical and military support from Germany in the Irish uprising against England in 1916. The mobilization of minds played a significant role in keeping up the morale of the troops, but above all, that of the people behind the frontline, who had to participate in the gigantic war effort. Moreover, the moral victory helped to attract neutral powers to their camp, especially the United States. Germany quickly lost on this ground and eventually became solely responsible for the First World War. An ostracized nation, Germany was humiliated at the end of the war and the attitude of the winners only served to sow the seeds of the Second World War (1939-1945).

SUMMARY

○── **1914**

7th-23rd Aug.: **Battle of the borders**
2nd Sept.: **German troops are 50km from Paris**
6th Sept.: **Start of the Battle of the Marne**
7th Sept.: **Operation "Taxis of the Marne"**
9th Sept.: **German retreat**
12th Sept.: **End of the Battle of the Marne**
14th-18th Sept.: **Battle of Aisne**
9th Oct.: **Capitulation of Antwerp metropolis**
29th Oct.: **Flooding of the plains of the Yser**
13th Nov.: **Stabilization of the front**

- The First World War was the result of deep and immediate causes, among which must be emphasized the economic, political and colonial tensions between the European powers, not to mention the building of alliances prompted by the fear of being attacked by rival countries. However, the spark that triggered the conflict was the assassination of the heir of Austria-Hungary in Sarajevo on 28 June 1914.

- Although the war seemed inevitable, it could have at least been limited to a regional scale. However, politicians and diplomats allowed things to evolve into a generalized conflict. The logic of alliances therefore created a domino effect and many states declared war on each other.

- The German and French staffs had long planned their attacks. The French decided to attack through Alsace-

Lorraine, while the Germans were planning to cross Belgium and attack the French armies from behind.

- Belgium was attacked on 4 August; the Belgian army quickly retreated to Antwerp. As for the French troops and the British Expeditionary Force, they fought on the Sambre and Mons. On 24 August, the battle of borders was won by Germany.
- The French armies had also failed in their offensive in the Ardennes and the Sarre, but they clung to the Meurthe.
- The German command then made the mistake of withdrawing its troops from the advancing wing and allowed itself to create gaps between the various armies.
- General Joseph Joffre, having perceived the weakness of the German device, took the opportunity to try to widen the spaces between the German armies and encircle them. General Helmuth von Moltke, who was in Luxemburg, was now unable to have an overall view and coordinate his troops.
- On 9 September, the German armies were obliged to retreat behind the Marne when they were just 50 kilometers from Paris.
- After an attempt in September and October to break the deadlock, the positions of the two armies remained frozen for nearly four years, thus initiating trench warfare.
- The first months of the war were marked by the surge of brutality. Contrary to popular belief, the battles of the borders and the Marne were the deadliest of the conflict.
- Civilians were not spared, despite the laws of war. The German army committed unforgivable acts in Belgium and northern France, torturing entire cities, committing massacres and destroying monuments.

FIND OUT MORE

BIBLIOGRAPHY

- Audoin-Rouzeau, S. and Becker, J.-J. (2004) *Encyclopédie de la Grande Guerre 1914-1918*. Paris: Bayard.
- Becker, J.-J. (2003) La bataille de la Marne ou la fin des illusions. *Les collections de L'Histoire*, Volume 21, pp. 32-36.
- Becker, J.-J. (2008) *Dictionnaire de la Grande Guerre*. Brussels: André Versaille.
- Contamine, H. (1970) *La victoire de la Marne. 9 septembre 1914*. Paris: Gallimard.
- Cochet, F. and Porte, R. (2008) *Dictionnaire de la Grande Guerre 1914-1918*. Paris: Robert Laffont.
- Duroselle, J.-B. (1994) *La Grande Guerre des Français (1914-1918)*. Paris: Perrin.
- Ferro, M. (2001) *The Great War: 1914-1918*. London: Routledge.
- Gambiez, F. and Suire, M. (1968) *Histoire de la Première Guerre mondiale. Crépuscule sur l'Europe*, Volume I. Paris: Fayard.
- Hirschfeld, G., Krumeich, G., Renz, I. and Pöhlmann, M. (2004) *Enzyklopädie Erster Weltkrieg*. Paderborn: Schöningh.
- Keegan, J. (1997) *La Première Guerre mondiale*. London: Pimlico.
- *À la une. Les grands événements du XXᵉ siècle et les journaux de l'époque* (1979) La bataille de la Marne. Paris: Atlas.
- Lagrange, F. (2005) *Inventaire de la Grande Guerre*. Paris:

Universalis.

- Le Naour, J.-Y. (2008) *Dictionnaire de la Grande Guerre.* Paris: Larousse.
- Neiberg, M. (2005) *Fighting the Great War. A Global History.* Cambridge: Harvard University Press.
- Renouvin, P. (1969) *La crise européenne et la Première Guerre mondiale.* Paris: Presses Universitaires de France.

ADDITIONAL SOURCES

- Blond, G. (2002) *The Marne: The Battle that Saved Paris and Changed the Course of the First World War.* London: Prion.
- Bourachot, A. (2014) *Marshal Joffre: The Triumphs, Failures and Controversies of France's Commander-in-Chief in the Great War.* Trans. Uffindell, A. Barnsley: Pen and Sword Military.
- Farr, D. (2008) *Mons 1914-1918: The Beginning and the End.* Solihull: Helion & Company Ltd.
- Perris, G.H. (2014) *France Turns the Tide: The Battle of the Marne 5-12 September 1914.* UK: Leonaur.
- Sumner, I. (2010) *The First Battle of the Marne 1914: The French 'Miracle' Halts the Germans.* Oxford: Osprey Publishing.
- Uffindell, A. (2013) *The Marne 1914: A Battlefield Guide.* Barnsley: Pen and Sword Military.
- Von Hausen, General M.C.L.F. (2015) *Memoirs of the Marne Campaign.* Pickle Partners Publishing.

ICONOGRAPHIC SOURCES

- Assassination of Archduke Franz Ferdinand of Hapsburg. © *Le Petit Journal*.
- Portrait of John Denton Pinkstone French. Royalty-free reproduction picture.
- Portrait of Joseph Joffre. Royalty-free reproduction picture.
- Portrait of Helmuth von Moltke. Royalty-free reproduction picture.
- German army in Belgium. © *Library of Congress*
- Marne taxis. © Jean-Pol Grandmont.

DOCUMENTARIES

- *The Battle of the Marne (1914)*. (2011) [Documentary]. Jean-François Cochet. Dir. France.

MUSEUMS AND COMMEMORATIVE BUILDINGS

- Reims Cathedral (France).
- Memorial of Charles Péguy and the Grande Tombe de Chauconin-Neufmontiers (France).
- Memorial of the Battle of the Marne in Dormans (France).
- National monument and museum of the victory of the Marne in Mondement (France).
- Museum of the Great War in Pays de Meaux (France).
- Trenches of Massiges (France).